LOVE
and
SURRENDER

LOVE *and* SURRENDER

New Teachings from Jesus

GINA LAKE

Endless Satsang Foundation
www.RadicalHappiness.com

Cover photographs:
© ThomasVogel /iStockPhoto.com

ISBN: 978-1502386441

Copyright © 2014 by Gina Lake

All rights reserved. No part of this book may be used or reproduced by any means, graphic, electronic, or mechanical, including photocopying, recording, taping, or by any information storage retrieval system without the written permission of the publisher except in the case of brief quotations embodied in critical articles and reviews.

Contents

Introduction   vii

Chapter 1: What Is Surrendered   1

Chapter 2: Surrendering the "I"   17

Chapter 3: Surrendering Fear   33

Chapter 4: Surrendering "I Want"   53

Chapter 5: Surrendering Knowing   69

Chapter 6: Surrendering to Love in Relationships   85

About the Author   113

INTRODUCTION

This is one in a trilogy of short books that focuses on freedom from the conditioned mind and opening the heart. This book, more than the other two (*Choice and Will* and *Beliefs, Emotions, and the Creation of Reality*), is about the spiritual Heart, the fountain of unconditional love, which was central to my teachings two thousand years ago. The other two books in the trilogy are important in understanding the power that the conditioned, or *egoic*, mind has in preventing people from experiencing this love that is at the core of everyone's being.

    Choice and will are what make it possible to move out of the negative and limiting beliefs of the false self, which prevent or curtail the possibility of living a fuller, happier, and more loving life. *Love and Surrender* explains what is necessary to be in the Heart—in one's divine Essence—and to live from there rather than from a more contracted ego-bound state of consciousness. Surrender is the mysterious thing that happens when one lets go of, or gives up, the perspective and beliefs of the false self for the true self. It is the "miracle" I have spoken of in other works of mine.

I do not speak to you now from any tradition, as I was never part of any tradition but belonged only to the Father. These words are for you today to help you find your way in today's world. If I don't sound as I have in the past, that is as it is meant to be, because the past is past. Today requires a teaching for today. Many of you are ready to hear the truth that is being expressed in these words and apply it in your lives.

My message today is the same as in times gone by: You are not only human but divine, and you are meant to flourish and love one another. You are no different than me. The gift the Father gives each of His children is the gift of His own divinity. He does not give it to only one son, but to all, even those who know Him not. He gives this gift freely and indiscriminately.

Love is the answer today, as it has always been, but love is more important than ever before because today you have the means to destroy this beautiful earth and all that live upon it. The obscurations to love need to be vanquished so that you can abide in peace on this planet. This is more imperative than ever, and so I have come to deliver this simple message of love. May you receive it in your heart and express it in your life.

Jesus, dictated to Gina Lake
October, 2014

Chapter 1

What Is Surrendered

Love and surrender are words that are often used in spiritual teachings. However, like so many words, what they point to cannot be expressed or contained in words, and so love and surrender are often misunderstood. When people think of love, they think of romantic or familial love, which is an emotion, a feeling. But the love I will be speaking of is more mysterious and pervasive than a feeling. This love is the ultimate in human attainment, while at the same time ever-present and therefore beyond any need for attainment, for you already have it.

Although ever-present, this love is often obscured, and therefore so often seems out of reach. It is here, though, and what is more true is that it is all that is here. This love is the vast sea, or ocean, of consciousness from which everything arises and of which everything is made. The love that I am describing is not only the substratum of life, but Life itself—God (if you will).

Love and surrender are important because they bring you your deepest heart's desire as a human being. You are meant to be happy, to love, to be at peace, and to be free. Those are the tasks, you could say, of these human lifetimes. You are meant to move from fear, hopelessness, anger, victimization, and hate to trust, strength, courage, joy, peace, and love.

This transformation comes about through surrender. All of the spiritual practices ever invented are designed to accomplish this one thing. Surrender is the boat that takes you from one shore to another, from the limited human experience to the experience of the Divine incarnate.

Surrender is the means by which you come to know Love, or God. Surrender is mysterious and often *not* something you do, but something that just happens when you cease doing certain things and cease efforting. As a result, surrender often happens when you don't expect it, when you are not trying to surrender and your attention is elsewhere. To some extent surrender is Grace, but a grace in which you play a part. You set the stage for Grace/surrender to happen. You invite it (intend it or pray for it), make room for it in your life, and recognize and allow it when it does happen. That is what you can do.

Because surrender is so mysterious and so critical to spiritual freedom, peace, happiness, and love, we are going to examine what surrender means, what is involved in it, and what is actually surrendered.

When people hear the word surrender, they usually think of one side surrendering to another in a war. The side that has surrendered has been defeated and disgraced and has lost something important, such as territory or rights, and those who have surrendered might be imprisoned or in some other way punished for having lost the war.

The surrender that I am referring to—spiritual surrender—has the opposite consequence, since spiritual surrender leads to gaining something, not losing something, and to greater freedom and happiness, not imprisonment and shame. In fact, what is lost and given up in spiritual surrender is imprisonment, limitation, fear, conflict, and suffering. Who wouldn't want to surrender under those circumstances?

The trouble is that spiritual surrender *feels* like you are giving up something you want and need for something unknown, uncertain, even scary, or for something that seems like nothing. Spiritual surrender *feels* like you are about to lose something even though you are about to gain something. Feelings sometimes lie! The trouble is that you don't discover what you have gained until *after* you have surrendered. Until then, surrender feels difficult.

Surrender feels difficult because you are attached to what needs to be surrendered, if only because it is the known, the familiar, even if it makes you unhappy. You cling to it out of habit. You don't want to surrender it. You struggle with surrendering it. Besides, what else is there?

What are the things that people struggle with surrendering that block them from love? Feelings, for one. You don't want to let go of your anger, your resentment, your hatred, or even your guilt, your shame, and your suffering. And yet, you don't know why you don't want to let go of these feelings. You just don't, and you may not even ask why.

Not wanting to let go of such feelings doesn't make sense, but the part of you that doesn't want to let go of a feeling is not rational. It doesn't choose based on what makes sense. It feels the way it feels, and it is attached to feeling this way, even if doing so doesn't make sense, even if doing so hurts and hurts others.

This irrational side of people is often what runs them, and it keeps them from questioning the thoughts and feelings that cause their suffering. Most people remain in the dark, letting their unconscious minds determine their choices and inner state. They are unwilling to shine the light of awareness onto their inner landscape.

In addition to their feelings, people also don't want to surrender their ideas about themselves and others, their judgments, their stories about the past, and their fantasies. People like these thoughts, or at least a part of them does, the less rational part. These are the thoughts that make you who you *think* you are—who you believe you are—but not who you *actually* are. They are also the thoughts that make you suffer.

It doesn't even occur to most people that they need to surrender these thoughts in order to be happy and more loving. No one else seems to be doing this either. Most people don't realize that these thoughts are the source of their suffering, their imprisonment in a small, limiting definition of themselves. Most people remain ignorant of their greater self, their true self, and so they huddle fearfully inside this shell created by their ideas about who they are, not realizing that they are in prison, not realizing what else is possible.

But you who are reading this do realize something that most others do not, or you wouldn't be reading this. You realize that life is meant to be richer, fuller, happier, and more loving. You realize that you can be happier and more loving, if only.... If only what? If only you are willing to surrender the familiar prison for the unfamiliar palace.

Before you can surrender what imprisons you, you have to realize that you are in prison and that a palace awaits you. That realization ignites the necessary willingness and conditions for surrender that take you from prison to palace, from fear to love, from limitation to happiness and fulfillment.

Surrender is essentially an exchange. You surrender the old for the new, since the two cannot coexist. One cancels out the other. Surrender cancels the old and makes it possible to discover something new. But first, the old must be surrendered. The old must be given up, let go of, and only then can you discover what takes its place.

Surrender requires faith that something will take the place of what was surrendered and faith that what takes its place will be better than what was given up. Usually, this faith comes naturally when the old way of being creates sufficient suffering.

I say "sufficient," because enormous suffering is often endured before most are willing to consider a new way of being, one that hasn't been modeled for them, one not taught in schools, a way of being that is different from the way most people are living. Very few are courageous enough to step outside the usual way of being without good cause, and that cause is most often deep suffering.

It isn't easy to go against the grain. Fortunately, there are more people today who are willing to do this, and those people are able to find and support each other in ways, through the internet and other means, like never before. So something else that must be surrendered is concern for what other people think, for their opinions of you. The madding crowd keeps everyone in line.

Most people are willingly, yet unconsciously, imprisoned and not looking for a way out. They are the waking and walking dead, going about their lives as they always have, following the rules, not looking within, not questioning the situation they find themselves in, not questioning why they and everyone else seem to be suffering. Their perspective on life is like everyone else's, and that perspective is good enough for them. It is the perspective of the ego, the false self.

For these individuals, spiritual surrender is not the issue because they don't realize the need for surrender. Their questions are: "How can I get more of what I want? How can I get so-and-so to do what I want? How can I get people to like me? How can I get…?" Their questions are about getting something for themselves, not about giving up something (surrender), least of all giving up their suffering and the self that needs and wants things for itself.

What such people don't understand is that everything that is of true value is gained through surrender and remains out of reach by refusing to surrender. This statement doesn't even make sense unless you realize what spiritual surrender refers to. You surrender the false self for the true self. You surrender one state of consciousness to gain another state of consciousness. You surrender your attachment to what causes you to be unhappy and unloving in order to become happy and loving.

This raises the question: What causes someone to be unhappy and unloving? Some believe that their happiness lies outside themselves, that it is caused by people, events, and things. But if you believe that, you are doomed to unhappiness, since you can never control people, events, and things enough to ensure your happiness.

This is also simply not true: Happiness is not dependent on people, events, and things. But most have to discover this for themselves. You are the maker of your own happiness; nobody and nothing else can make you happy. And you are the one who determines to what extent you experience love in your life.

No one and no thing can make you feel happy, and no one and no thing can make you feel love or loved, at least not for long. You have the power within you to be happy and be loving, just as you have the power to be unhappy and unloving. Surrender is what takes you from unhappy and unloving to happy and loving. So let us look more closely at what needs to be surrendered for this transformation to take place.

Most essentially, the "I" must be surrendered. It must be laid at the feet of the Father. You offer the "I" up (surrender it) to God. This could not be done if there weren't something here capable of doing this, which is the true "I," the true self. The true self offers up the false self, and in so doing, becomes free of the false self and the suffering it creates.

The false self is every idea you have about yourself, every *thought* that begins with "I" and every other thought that relates to "I." Yes, every one. The true self has no need for such thoughts. It just is. It is what is alive in you and experiences life. The true self has no need to define or limit itself with words, while words are all the false self has.

The false self is nothing but the words that it describes itself as: "I am this, I am that, I am not this, I am not that." The false self is a limited self: Some definitions are included, while others are left out. This is not the experience of the true self of itself, which is boundless, all-inclusive, and without definition. Anything you might say about the true self would be incomplete and therefore untrue.

Before you understand this about your true nature, you must experience this for yourself. Some experience of the spacious, all-embracing nature of the true self is necessary before the false self can be surrendered. Even then, this surrender is an ongoing, moment-to-moment process, a moment-to-moment choice. As long as you are human, you are never really finished surrendering.

In every moment, the false self coexists with the true self. The false self exists as thoughts about yourself, while the true self exists as the experience you are having, including the experience of thought. Thoughts put you at the center of the universe and make the universe about *you* instead of you *being* the universe, which is more the truth.

When you become involved in your thoughts about yourself, you are involved with the false self; when you are not, you drop into the pure experience of the moment. The sense of "I" drops away and you become the universe. When you let yourself be nothing, you realize yourself as everything. These are two very different ways of being!

Experiencing the moment without involvement in thoughts about yourself and your life allows you to know your true nature. If you stay in that experience long enough, you will feel love, peace, contentment, beauty, gratitude, awe, and joy, because that is the true self's experience of life. But since few people are able to stay mentally quiet long enough to experience the depths of the true self, these moments of beauty and joy tend to be fleeting, while the experience of absorption in the self-centeredness of the false self is most people's ongoing experience.

Identification with the false self would not be a problem if living as if you were the center of the universe were a pleasant and effective way to live your life—if it worked! But it isn't and it doesn't. That state of mind, the state of identification with one's mental commentary, with one's ego, generally produces an experience of life that is quite the opposite of the true self's experience of life: Instead of peace, your thoughts create anger, conflict, and confusion. Instead of love, your thoughts create blame, hatred, jealousy, envy, and resentment. Instead of joy, contentment, and gratitude, your thoughts create discontentment, unhappiness, greed, and envy. These two states—the state of consciousness that is the false self and the state of consciousness that is the true self—are worlds apart.

What Is Surrendered

Surrender is the bridge that takes you from one world to the other.

To make this leap from one world to another, something else must be surrendered: fear. Fear is like a guard at the exit door of the false self's world: Whenever you approach the door that leads to the world of the true self, you are told that you can't go there. Fear is the guard that keeps you in your place, a place of compliant, unconscious suffering.

Fear masquerades as a guard, as someone who is trying to protect you from what is beyond the door, from the unknown, but he is actually the warden who maintains your imprisonment. He keeps you from the Father's palace, while pretending there is something terrible on the other side of the door. It takes courage, trust, and faith to surrender this fear and walk past the guard.

People are also kept in the false self's world by their desires. These are the baubles dangled temptingly before you, designed for your pleasure and for keeping you happy amidst your suffering. But the happiness they deliver never lasts for long, hence the need for another desire and another. There is no end to the false self's desires, since the false self is never satisfied.

Fulfilling these desires keeps people busy and keeps them from looking within and questioning their suffering and way of life. Chasing after one desire and then another keeps you occupied and pretending that you will be happy when.... People exchange happiness *now* for discontentment and striving and the promise of happiness in the future. The false self's desires are designed to keep you on a treadmill of activity, always reaching for something ahead, while missing the beauty and perfection of life as it is unfolding right now.

Surrendering the desires of the false self does not mean surrendering all desire, however, as deeper desires drive the true self. The true self's desires are felt quite differently than those of the false self. These deeper desires are what is surrendered *to*. You exchange the false self's desires for truer, more meaningful ones. You surrender to a higher desire, a higher will.

These desires are the will of the Father, not the will of the ego. You exchange your personal will for Thy will. When you do that, your activity and actions become joyous, fluid, balanced, and kind to yourself and others. You are freed from creating negativity and therefore, for the most part, from experiencing negativity. And whatever negativity you do experience does not affect you as it did in the past.

Once you have put your life and actions in the hands of the Father, your hands are free to give of yourself and to enjoy all that you do. They are no longer tied to unfulfilling activities out of duty to conformity and other people's expectations. The Father's bidding is always good and brings happiness to all. This is a different world, indeed, than that of the false self.

The final thing that must be surrendered is what you think you know, for to enter the Father's palace, requires that you be naked in the moment, free of all pretense of knowing who you are, who others are, what will be, why things were as they were, and why they are as they are. When you are stripped this bare, then it is possible for you to know what cannot be put into words and to have access to everything you need to know—for that moment.

Chapter 2

Surrendering the "I"

If you pay close attention to your thoughts, you will quickly see that they revolve around "I." Most thoughts are about yourself or are being thought because they have some importance and relevance to "I." Most of the time, what goes through your mind is a dialog between you and you about you or things of interest to you. You are very important to you!

Even thoughts about others ultimately relate back to you and your relationship with them: How do they feel about you? How do they or did they affect you? How will they affect you when…? What do you like or not like about them? What do you think of them?

All of this rumination related to you creates a sense of yourself in relation to others and to the world. This sense of yourself is what I am calling the false self. It is, after all, just a *sense* of yourself. It isn't anything more than that. It cannot pick up your groceries or put your kids to bed.

Something else is actually living your life, doing all the things necessary to sustain your life, and that mysterious but very real something does not need a sense of yourself to do those things. In fact, as you well know, that sense of yourself could be very different from what it is right now and you would still exist and do things.

That sense of self is infused, or colored, by ideas, beliefs, and images and connected to a particular body-mind, all of which further flesh out this sense of self, making it appear more solid and real than it actually is. This sense of self seems so real and its ideas, beliefs, and images seem so true that it influences what you do, how you do things, when you do them, and if you do them at all.

But that sense of self doesn't have to affect any of your activities or how you live your life. On some level, it is a choice to have your sense of self affect your existence and your activities to the extent that it does. What a radical idea that is! It is, of course, completely natural for that sense of self to influence your life. Human beings are designed to have a sense of self that seems to be real and seems to be who they are. They are designed to play the part of a specific character, although that character is not who they really are.

Nevertheless, do you see that there is some choice in how much and in what way that sense of self affects your life? Your life, after all, is yours. You are not the character, and your life does not belong to the sense of self. The sense of self is just a sense, and it can change. It can even fall into the background, in which case, the real you, the one that is living your life, will barely be influenced by it.

Ideas and images, which is essentially what the sense of self is, can only affect you to the extent that you allow them to and to the extent that you are unconscious of them. You don't necessarily let other people's ideas affect you, but when those ideas come from your own mind, that is a different matter. Those seem real and true—they seem meaningful to *you*. But they are only meaningful in that they create the false you, a pretend you, a mirage that seems like you.

This wouldn't be a problem if the sense of self and all of its ideas were not also the source of human suffering, because many of the ideas are negative, limiting, and simply untrue and because the sense of self, itself, is false. How can a false self and false and limiting ideas lead to happiness, peace, and love? Lies can only lead to suffering and take you away from the truth. And so they do.

The problem with the false self is that it keeps you from recognizing your true nature and the truth about life, both of which are good news. The false self keeps you bound within a certain perception, one that causes suffering. The false self sees the world from a lens of fear, distrust, lack, and competition. It is essentially an unhappy, discontent, egocentric, and fearful self.

Something else is here that is much more than just a sense of yourself and all the ideas that go along with that. It uses the body-mind to get about and accomplish things, but the body-mind would be useless and inert without it. What is this mysterious thing that is alive within your body-mind, sensing through it, and moving it about? That is the true self. It is called by many names: the Divine Self, Essence, Spirit, Consciousness, Awareness, the Holy Spirit,

Being, the Higher Self, and the Pearl Beyond Price, just to name a few.

The title of this chapter, "Surrendering the 'I,'" points to the possibility of not allowing the sense of self—the false self—to shape your life and determine your choices but allowing something else that is real and much wiser and more loving to shape your life, something that has already been shaping your life to some extent.

This mysterious something—the real you—allows your life to be shaped by the false self and its ideas until you wake up to the realization that you are more than this. How momentous this is, when you first realize that you can wake up from the prison created by the false self and live more from the indwelling Spirit! And what a great mystery this business of being human is! What wakes up? What sees the truth about who you are? Who are you? What are you?

As I said earlier, before you can be released from the prison of the false self, you first must realize that you are in prison. Getting to that point takes three things: willingness, awareness, and choice. You have to be willing to look (so many are not!) and then you have to actually look. You have to choose to turn the spotlight of your attention onto something that most people don't want to look at or don't bother to look at: their own mind.

Isn't it interesting that the objectivity that is felt to be so important in observing the outer world is rarely turned in on one's own mind? Rarely do you run across someone who suggests doing this. Even psychotherapists who ask their clients to look within usually assume that a client's thoughts and feelings are a true representation of who he or she is, without acknowledging that such thoughts and feelings are part of the mirage of being human and must be looked beyond to discover the real truth. But there is a place for that kind of examination, of course, and this is by no means intended as an indictment of psychotherapy.

As long as the sense of self is felt to be the real self, the experience of the real self will be only fleeting and not recognized. The real self will remain in the background, unacknowledged and therefore not experienced as such. Of course it is impossible to not experience the real self, because the real self is what is reading these words and experiencing life. It is the only thing that is experiencing and can experience life.

The human condition is such that people assume that something else is the real self. They assume that the false self is the real self, that it is the experiencer, the wise one, and what acts. The reality is that the false self (your thoughts) only pretends to be wise and to know things that cannot be known, while true wisdom flows from the depths of the real self and is overlooked by the false self. And actions, which could come entirely from the real self are often determined by the false self instead, which barks out commands and seeks to control your every behavior: "Do this now. Do it better. Hurry Up. You'll never get it done in time."

Much of the commentary that goes through people's minds is a chain of thoughts designed to get them to take action in directions that will yield greater power, control, safety, security, pleasure, recognition, and comfort, all things the ego esteems. There is nothing wrong with these things, but there is much more to life. The false self doesn't know how to create a happy, loving life. The life it creates is lopsided and detached from what brings true meaning to life.

Through some kind of mutiny, the egoic mind (the voice in your head) has become the captain of this ship of the body-mind, while the real captain has been sequestered down below. He has been replaced by a less capable captain whose guiding principles are fear, power, selfishness, and control. This false master is not a good master. He is not wise and he is not kind. Reinstating the wise and kind master so that love and right action can reign once again on board is the goal of spiritual evolution.

Surrendering the "I" is impossible without first recognizing the need for surrender. You have to have clearly seen the ineptness and destructiveness of your thoughts. This takes not only awareness of your thoughts, but also the willingness to examine and question them.

Surrendering the "I" is also not possible until you are fed up with the current master and open to noticing the real you, which has been patiently waiting for you to be done with the drama of the false self. Do you long for the goodness of your true nature? Do you long for God? Do you long to be done with the suffering caused by your judgments, mistaken beliefs, and negative feelings? Do you want peace and love more than you want your thoughts about yourself? Who or what would you be without your thoughts about you? Are you willing to discover this? The strength of your willingness and longing to be free of suffering and to know God will determine your readiness and ability to surrender.

Let's take a look at what is involved in surrendering the "I." Let's say that you find yourself caught up in a thought that makes you angry: "She shouldn't have done that to me!" Before you can surrender your (the false self's) anger, you first have to see that both the thought and the anger originated in the sense of "I."

The "I" has an idea about how people should and shouldn't behave. When someone doesn't comply with that belief, you feel angry. Did the person make you angry or did your belief? Your belief did. The "I" made the "I" angry. Do you want to feel angry? If not, the only way out is to surrender the belief that caused the anger. How do you do that? What is involved in surrendering a belief?

A belief is a thought, and a thought can only remain in existence if you give it attention. If you give a thought attention, you breathe life into it. Beliefs are thoughts that you have given so much attention to that you now firmly believe them. Without your attention, a thought cannot live for very long, and without your repeated attention, a thought cannot become a belief. You are very powerful! You animate and maintain the false self with your attention. You breathe life into the false self by giving your thoughts repeated attention. Without this attention, thoughts wither and beliefs fade away.

Furthermore, since you have to put your attention somewhere, when you withdraw it from a thought, your attention will breathe life into something else. What else might you enliven and sustain with your attention? If you put your attention on a flower, for instance, you will have the experience of the flower. If you hold your attention there long enough, you will feel a sense of merging with the flower and the joy that comes with that simple, yet profound experience.

What do you prefer: anger or the joy of fully experiencing a flower? You get to choose. Giving your attention fully to anything other than thoughts about yourself produces joy, peace, love and contentment. When you do that, you are no longer in the world of the false self but have entered the world of the true self, which is a world of unity with all life. You have moved from the prison of the ego to the Father's palace.

To the mind this sounds overly simplistic and not at all practical. And yet, giving attention to a flower or anything else that is real within your sensory environment is much more practical—functional—than giving attention to any thought you might have about you and your life, which at best serves no function at all and at worst serves a negative one.

"Blasphemy!" says the mind. "How dare you tamper with the cult of the mind, the cult of the *me*. How dare you attempt to break the spell of the false self!" That is exactly what happens every time you refuse to feed a thought about yourself or any other thought that maintains the false self, such as a fearful thought or an egoic desire. Fear is in place to keep you from leaving your egoic mind behind. That is fear's job, and it will not quiet down easily. So you will have to surrender fear as well.

What power you have in attention! You create your experience of life with nothing more than your attention. Life allows you to create in this way. It allows you to have the experience you choose to create. You can have a life that is lost in the drama and pain of the false self or one that is an expression of the true self. It is your choice.

Surrendering the "I" and its beliefs is more of a not-doing than a doing. You cease doing what you normally and automatically do, which is feed a thought with your attention and more thoughts. Surrender feels like a sacrifice, a letting go of something you want, because people are naturally attached to doing what they have always done: think and believe their thoughts. Surrender is difficult because it feels like you have to give up something you love doing (thinking) for nothing, while quite the opposite is true.

The key to surrender is becoming aware of your *attachment* to a thought or feeling—to how much you want to be involved with it, even if that thought or feeling is not pleasant. Notice the pull that a thought or a feeling has on you and the sense of *needing* to be involved with it. In some cases, you may feel like you won't survive if you don't pay attention to a particular thought. This is especially the case when fear is involved.

When you are caught up in a thought or feeling, stop and take a few moments to let yourself explore and get to know the experience of that, including how a part of you enjoys feeling bad. The feeling of attachment is quite tangible, almost real. That is how convincing the mirage is. The attachment feels real, powerful, and difficult to let go of.

When you are under the influence of the attachment, it's got you. You are convinced that it is powerful and difficult to let go of. But when you just stop a moment and let yourself feel the attachment fully, something very interesting happens: The attachment loosens, and it is seen for what it is—a mirage, an illusion.

That which sees the illusion is not part of the illusion. It is the real self. When you choose to stop a moment and feel your attachment to a thought or feeling, what is able to do that is the real self. At that point, your real self has taken over and is being used to investigate the false self. The true captain is back on deck. Then you have a choice: You can go back to that train of thought or put your attention on something other than thoughts. The more you practice this, the easier it becomes to move beyond the egoic mind, the originator of the false self, and to know your true self.

Specifically, here are the steps involved in surrender. These steps are what you can do to *not* do what is conditioned and automatic, which is to get lost in thought:

1. Notice that you are caught up in a thought, a train of thoughts, or a feeling.

2. Gently tell yourself, "Stop." This breaks the egoic trance, the spell of the illusion. The pause provides an opportunity to make a choice between continuing to think or surrendering thinking.

3. During this pause, notice any attachment or desire to going back to that thought or feeling. It can help to mentally label it: "Attachment, desire to think." Feel free to name or describe it in whatever way makes the most sense to you.

4. Take a moment to feel that attachment in your body and more subtly energetically. Where is it located? In your gut? Heart? Head? Throat? Stomach? What does it feel like? Tight? Dark? Sticky? Grasping? Empty? Churning? Explore it. Examine it. Just be with the physical and energetic sense of it for a while with curiosity and interest.

5. Accept the attachment. Don't be upset about it or judge it. Being attached to thinking the

thoughts that go through your mind is part of being human. There has never been a human who has not had such thoughts and been attached to them. As long as you are in a human body, it cannot be otherwise. But such attachments don't have to control where your attention goes. Once you are aware of being attached to a particular thought or feeling, you have a choice.

6. Next, broaden your awareness to include whatever else is present besides thoughts, feelings, and attachment to them. Look around you. Experience your environment through your senses. Notice what else is part of this moment in time. Is the sun shining? What sensations are you experiencing? What sounds do you hear? What are you aware of in your environment?

7. Now notice what is present on a more subtle level. The subtle level is the level in which the true self resides, and it is accessed by becoming aware of your sensory experience: Is love present? Peace? Relaxation? Awe? Compassion? A sense of beauty? Can you experience any of these even

just a little? What is the experience like? Can you feel the aliveness that is the signature of your true self?

8. Give your attention more fully to the love, peace, joy, compassion, and acceptance of the true self, and you will come to know yourself as those qualities instead of as the false self. Over time, your ability to sense the subtle world of the true self will increase, and you will begin to live increasingly as your true self.

Surrender has a great reward, and that reward is love. When you surrender being lost in thought, you discover a new world, a subtle but more real world, which has been there all along, awaiting your notice and appreciation. You are what experiences this real world *and* you are everything you experience as well. That is the great mystery that is *you!*

Chapter 3

Surrendering Fear

The conditioned self, the false self, is run by fear and maintained by fear, which is the antithesis of love. Fear and love are at odds because fear distrusts and rejects life, while love trusts and embraces life. Therefore, fear and love cannot coexist. They represent points of view that do not intersect; either one or the other prevails.

Fear is the point of view of the ego, the primitive, conditioned aspect of yourself, which is largely what makes you human. Without an ego, people would readily experience their indwelling Spirit and the love it has for all life. With the ego, people experience fear, and because they do, they are driven to conquer, control, and dominate their environment and other human beings. The underlying belief driving the ego's behavior is "eat or be eaten." The ego's solution to the problem of survival is to conquer, be on top, vanquish. In pursuit of this, the ego seeks power, recognition, strength, beauty, and intelligence. If it attains these things, the ego believes that comfort, food, sex, safety, security, and happiness will be ensured.

Notice the absence of the word love in this description of the ego. There is no room for love in the ego's world unless love is seen as a means for achieving the ego's goals. Otherwise, love is presumed to be a potential weakness, a vulnerability. In love you let your guard down, you must trust someone not to hurt you, and you must share and compromise with another, all things that are abhorrent to the ego.

Until a person gains some mastery over the ego, his or her relationships are doomed to difficulty and dysfunction, because the ego is the enemy of love. The ego knows nothing about love, it does not value love, and it undermines and destroys love within oneself and in one's relationships.

Fear is what makes the ego what it is, and fear is what keeps someone from recognizing that he or she is something other than the false self. Until there is at least some recognition and involvement with the true self, there can be no happiness, for happiness and fear are mutually exclusive, just as love and fear are. True happiness comes from connection with one's true nature, with the love and peace at your core, not from getting or from dominating, which is the ego's strategy for happiness.

Because fear is so intimately tied to the ego, it is impossible to see past the ego until you have overcome fear to some degree. Those who have grown up in an unsafe or a threatening family or environment have great difficulty getting beyond their fear and, therefore, have difficulty relaxing into the love and peace of their true nature. They are forever on guard for the next attack, the next reproach.

While many live in such an environment today, most of you who are reading this do not live, at least any longer, in a punitive or unloving home or in a war zone. You are, for the most part, safe from immediate threats. And yet, even the safest and most comfortable of you suffers to some degree from various fears: fear of aging, ill health, poverty, loneliness, and death. Regardless of your situation in life, these are universal fears that must be dealt with.

I am here to help you surrender these universal fears, to help you trust, relax, and return to your true nature. I am here to deliver the message that not only do you have love and peace at your core, but so does the Intelligence behind all life: the Father. Do you believe this? If you did, how would this change how you feel and how you are in your life?

Take a moment, if you will, to take a deep breath and relax into the comfort of wherever you are. With each breath, allow yourself to sink more deeply into that comfort, that safety of whatever is holding you up. Allow yourself to feel how you are being supported by whatever is supporting you. Let yourself fully experience being held and supported. You are safe. You are here, and Life is supporting your existence here and now. In this moment, as in every moment, you are being taken care of.

It is a miracle, isn't it, how you arrived at this moment in time? And at every step of the way, in every moment, your existence was supported: by people, by opportunities, by things, by information, by guidance, by your own talents, by your intelligence, and by the magnificent miracle that is your body.

And in the next moment you will be supported and in the next, until you reach a time when your body no longer sustains you and you discover that you never needed your body to exist, as you continue to be nourished and supported in other dimensions—for eternity! There is no end to your existence, your power, your beauty. If you only knew how magnificent and powerful you are!

If you could more fully experience your eternal nature, you would easily embrace this life, which is so fleeting and so precious. From the standpoint of your true nature, this human experience is immeasurably valuable and treasured for the opportunities it provides for growth and for serving others.

You are going through whatever you are going through on this planet, in this dimension, for a reason—for many, many reasons, all of them purposeful, all of them worthwhile but which you may not understand. When you leave your mortal body, you continue to exist, and you take with you all the wisdom, knowledge, and talents you have acquired into the next adventure, the next stage of your existence.

From the standpoint of your soul, earth is the greatest of schools, like none other, and this lifetime is a grand and heroic undertaking. Your soul willingly embraces all manner of challenges you face here—all of them. Your soul has the strength and resources to benefit from every possible experience, regardless of how painful. And your soul has the power to heal every experience and be transformed by every experience.

If only you knew and could fully feel the excitement, enthusiasm, and joy that your soul feels for this gift of being alive now on earth. When you are able to step out of the ego's point of view, you can feel the love, wonderment, awe, and gratitude of your soul for this life. This is why it is so important to learn to move beyond the false self—because your life *can* be experienced as a blessing, as a precious gift.

It is possible even in this moment—right now—to feel this, simply by stopping to notice the love, joy, awe, and gratitude that are here right now. Are you willing to take a moment to do that? What might prevent you from doing that? Isn't it only a thought that would prevent this? Notice that thought, if it is there, and then turn away from it and turn your attention to the experience of this sweet moment. Stay with this experience long enough to feel the subtle happiness of your true self. Can you feel it, even just a little? The more you allow yourself to feel this, the more it becomes your reality.

This moment was designed just for you as a vehicle for experiencing the love that is within your heart. How else could God experience love as a human being unless God became one? How else could God experience such an adventure as this life without creating such a world as this? Can you feel God's pleasure in this, in His/Her creation, and the excitement of what might be discovered and learned from this unique place and moment in time?

Nowhere else in the universe is there a planet like this one. And nowhere else is there a person like you or circumstances like the ones you find yourself in. How quickly it all passes! From the standpoint of eternity, this life passes in the blink of an eye. One day, it will feel like that to you too. This lifetime will be but a vague memory, a story about someone you were long ago. Realizing how ephemeral and precious this life is will help you to cope with life's challenges, which are made much more difficult than they need to be by the ego.

Move out of the false self and discover the rich resources offered by your divine Self for overcoming and learning from your challenges. If you turn to the ego instead, you will get stuck in suffering. But something else knows the way out of all suffering. This mysterious something is your salvation, your means for happiness and peace. But you must turn to it, choose it, get to know it, and learn to live from it. It is who you really are. You know when you have found it because it feels like arriving home. You know it by the love you feel in your heart and by the "peace that passeth all understanding."

When you feel this love and peace, know that you have found your way Home and that this is how life is meant to feel. You are not meant to suffer, except when you are aligned with the ego and believing the ego's perceptions. Suffering is how you are shown what is false, what *not* to believe, what *not* to trust. You can trust your suffering to show you what is false in this world, and you can trust love and peace to show you what is true and trustworthy.

Always go in the direction of love, and you cannot go wrong. This is the simple compass you have been given to point you Homeward. As long as you listen to your thoughts, it will be difficult to find your way. You will suffer and be confused. But when you stop listening to your thoughts, you will find freedom, peace, and happiness, and your heart will be full of love, gratitude, and awe.

Fear is the great hurdle. Fear keeps you in your suffering. Fear keeps you believing what your thoughts tell you about yourself, about others, about life—all lies, or nearly so. When you look, you discover that so little in your thoughts is true and helpful, so little, in fact, that you will never miss your thoughts about yourself and your life. They have never helped you find your way but only caused you to lose your way.

But how can I convince the fearful mind? You must convince yourself by seeing for yourself the truth of what I am saying. Look at what you are thinking. Are your thoughts true, helpful, and wise? Or are they confused, unkind, petty, and largely untrue? Don't your thoughts argue both sides of an issue? One day you are on one side of an issue or a choice, and the next day you are on the other side. Following the voice in your head is like riding in a boat without a rudder: It moves forward but with no clear direction, or it spins around in circles.

All the while, the mind is full of judgment, anger, complaints, and pettiness, rarely happy, rarely content. There is no peace, no relaxation, no gratitude, no contentment, no love when you listen to your thoughts. They never let you rest: You are never good enough. Life is never good enough. Others are never good enough.

Feel the tension and contraction in your body when you think your thoughts. That tells you something about them. That contraction is a form of suffering. It is a sign of disconnection from your source and a sign that you need to align with something truer and more real than the voice in your head.

What else is here? How do you experience the still, small voice within? How can you experience your sweet Self? You experience it by saying no to that which takes you away from it, by saying no to your thoughts, particularly to your thoughts of fear. And then you listen for that still, small voice, patiently. You make room for it, you wait for it, and you allow it to be heard.

Your fears are fantasies or, more accurately, nightmarish illusions. Your mind makes your fears up, and then the feelings they create in your body convince you that your fears are real—but they are not! They are imaginations rather than what is or what will be. Your fears are no more true or real than the monsters in novels or movies. Your fears are created by your ego to keep you listening to it. That is all they are. That is their sole purpose.

It may be that the things you fear have happened to someone at some time in the universe. But to assume that what you fear will happen to you is a leap of faith—faith in a fantasy. If only you had as much faith in the truth, which is that you have the inner resources for dealing with your challenges and that every challenge serves a purpose in your growth. Furthermore, every challenge has a gift to offer, and how much you suffer in the face of a challenge depends on how much you listen to your thoughts.

Some of the most compelling fears are fears of poverty, illness, pain, disability, and death. It is natural to be afraid of these things. The mind is programmed to contemplate worst-case scenarios. However, doing this is not as functional as it may seem. Having these fears and examining such possibilities does not prevent or protect you from experiencing what you fear. Being afraid of something also doesn't cause it to happen. There is no magic in fearful thoughts. A fearful thought has nothing to do with what actually happens and doesn't actually help you cope with whatever does happen.

Do you see that such fears do not arise as a prediction or forewarning of an actual event? You have had many, many fears in your lifetime, and they have not manifested. Fearful thoughts arise regularly, spontaneously, and randomly, often without a connection to anything real.

When fearful thoughts are connected to an event, such as a toothache or job loss, the mind tends to pile on more fearful thoughts, which increase the fear and other unpleasant emotions. Without the fear and confusion of the egoic mind, what are you left with in the face of a toothache, a job loss, a diagnosis, or some other difficulty? You are left with this moment, which is all you ever have. You always have only this moment and this moment's experience. And that is where the solution to your so-called problems lies.

If some pain or other problem is calling for your attention, then you do what you can about it. You take steps. If this is not a moment for taking steps, then leave all thoughts about the problem alone. Do not pick those thoughts up and run with them. Do not think about what might happen, what the problem might mean, or how it might affect you. Do you see how useless these types of thoughts are? They do not lead to answers and they don't change a thing.

Even thinking about what to do about a problem is not where the solution lies. The mind will spin around in circles, trying to figure out what to do, but the best answers come from deep inside: At a certain point, you just *know* what to do or you find yourself inspired to take a particular action.

Your true self will take care of you if you give it a chance to. But you must listen to something other than your thoughts. You must listen to the communications of the true self, which are more subtle than the thoughts in your head. The true self communicates through intuition, knowings, inspiration, and urges to act. Unfortunately, the thoughts set in motion by the fearful thoughts produce additional emotions and exhaustion, making it more difficult to function and tune in to the true self's subtle communications.

This over-involvement with the mind and emotions leaves people feeling hopeless, powerless, and bad about their life. The false self takes an experience, like an illness or a job loss, and puts itself at the center of a story about it: "This always happens to me. Just when I was doing so well. Now this. I can never get on top of things." Such storytelling about one's life only magnifies the fear, unhappiness, and pain. It causes unnecessary suffering.

Why would you want to increase your pain this way? I am sure you don't, and you don't have to once you are aware of how the egoic mind creates suffering whenever something happens that it doesn't like: "My life is not supposed to go this way! Life is unfair. I never get what I want." That kind of thinking never serves. Life goes as it goes, and everyone must learn to take whatever life brings in stride, which is to say, accept things the way they are and not take them personally.

To enter the Father's palace, you must surrender to your life as it is. You must surrender "your life," that is, the story of your life. And you must surrender your fears about what may be. You must leave them behind. There is no need for such fears where you are going (Home, to the present moment). You never needed your fears anyway, which is what you discover if you can trust enough to move beyond them.

The key to overcoming your fearful thoughts is staying in the present moment. Fearful thoughts are by nature thoughts about the future—a possible frightening future. This future doesn't and never will exist, although the mind makes such thoughts seem real and important. They are an illusion. The only thing that is real is your present moment experience, the experience you are having right *now*.

Under even the most difficult circumstances, if you are able to be in the here and now rather than in your thoughts *about* it and take life one moment at a time, you will discover that you have the resources for dealing with any challenge.

When people get caught up in their thoughts and feelings, they lose access to their inner resources. Fear activates the body's fight-or-flight response, which deactivates the part of the brain that helps you reason and tap in to your intuition. So being caught in thoughts and feelings of fear is more of an immobilizing state than a helpful one.

To access the part of your brain that you need for overcoming challenges, your rational mind and your inner wisdom, you need to surrender your thoughts and fears and become very present in the here and now. When you do that, the physiological effects of fear disappear, and you are capable of taking wise action, if action is needed.

Turning your attention to what you are experiencing here and now, in the present moment, vanquishes all fear. From this place, it is easy to see your life more clearly, from the perspective of the true self. When you stay in the here and now, not only do you gain access to wisdom and right action, but you also realize you are eternal and being supported by a loving universe in which you are deeply cared for. You feel grateful for existing in this moment and curious and interested in what may happen next.

The state of mind, or consciousness, that is the true self is as different from the state of mind of the false self as night is to day. It is like waking up from a nightmare into a beautiful, loving, caring world. Fear creates the nightmare and sustains it. Seeing that fear is an illusion and serves no positive purpose frees you from having to experience the nightmare caused by unnecessary fear.

What you discover is that you never needed any thoughts about the future, because the future takes care of itself when you allow yourself to be fully present in the here and now, where you really exist. The false self exists in the past and future, as an idea of yourself, but the true self inhabits the present— alone, for the false self cannot exist in the present moment. The false self dissolves as soon as you land in the present moment. Then all that exists is the wonderment, awe, beauty, love, peace, and joy of your true self.

Because people rarely stay in the present moment for long before their thoughts catch them up once again, this description of the present moment may sound unrealistic and unattainable. But it is not. Everyone is destined to discover the power of the present moment and that of their true self.

Surrendering fear is key in this discovery, as fear is the monster at the gate that leads to the Father's palace. But the monster is an illusion! Fortunately, you don't even have to fight with an illusion to overcome it. All you need to do is realize that it is an illusion. Fear is an illusion! Are you willing to trust this? Surrendering fear requires trusting that the monsters of the mind are illusions and then being willing to walk past them and enter the palace of the present moment.

Many a hero in myths and legends has been in this position. The hero sends out a call or prayer for help in getting past the monster at the gate, after which aid appears in some form, possibly simply as an idea or inspiration to do something. When you are faced with a fear that you are convinced is true, send out a call or prayer for help and know that it will be answered. The hero always succeeds, but never solely by virtue of his own strength, but with the help of the gods. Do ask, and you shall receive. Know this. It is a law of life.

Ask for help and then surrender your fear to the Father. Put it in His hands, give it to Him, and let it be His "problem." So often, it is feelings of powerlessness and hopelessness that keep people stuck in their thoughts and fears. Surrender these feelings too to the Father, put them at His feet, in His hands, and let Him take care of what seems too big or difficult for you to handle by yourself. You see, you are never alone, unless you choose to be. Each person has the strength of the universe behind him or her, if you but ask for it.

Chapter 4

Surrendering "I Want"

One of the most compelling "I" thoughts is the thought "I want." People love to think about what they want. Their desires are food for fantasies about their future life, as if all you had to do was mentally design a future life and then step into it and live it. This is how the ego seems to believe life is shaped or *should* be shaped, without acknowledging that something else much more powerful, which trumps the personal will, is shaping life alongside the ego's desires.

One's desires are not as powerful as the ego supposes or wishes them to be, and this is the cause of much unhappiness, dissatisfaction, and anger. If you agree with the ego's perception that life should comply or you should be able to get it to comply with your desires, you will be sorely disappointed, for although life sometimes does do this, it often does not, no matter how strongly you desire something or how much you apply yourself to getting it. There is no magic formula for getting what you want because there is a larger force, a greater will, that ultimately determines whether you do or not.

This is not good news to the ego. Its desires are extremely important to it. Getting what it wants is the ego's strategy for survival, for keeping safe and finding some security in this "perilous" world. The ego is afraid of the world, so it sets out to get certain things for itself to ensure its safety and happiness.

Who can blame it? When the world is seen through the ego's eyes, this makes perfect sense. The problem is that the world is not as the ego perceives it to be, and so the ego's strategy is flawed. A strategy that is based on misperceptions or only part of the truth is bound to not be very useful and may, in fact, lead to poor results. And so it does.

Trying to create a life as you imagine it when life is not designed to give you that can only lead to frustration and unhappiness. Life has its own design and reason for being, and that reason is not to give your ego what it wants, although the ego does sometimes get what it wants.

The ego is not meant to be the master creator of your life. It is the aspect of the human being that creates conflict, unpleasant emotions, complications, confusion, and bad karma. How can something like that create a beautiful and fulfilling life? And yet, that is what is at the helm of most people's lives.

No wonder there is so much suffering and unhappiness in this world: At the helm is a rather diabolical aspect of the human being, not the divine aspect. The ego is the villain in the human drama. Fortunately, the Divine is ultimately what is in control of life, not the ego. The Divine allows the ego to have some control because this leads to lessons and consequently to growth, which is part of the divine design.

The ego's desires, then, are misguided, because what is behind such desires is not wise enough to know what is best for oneself, only what is assumed to be best based on the ego's misunderstandings about life and about what makes for happiness.

The problem is that the ego's perceptions are skewed by fear. Every fear the false self has becomes a desire:

The false self fears powerlessness, so it desires power over others, not realizing that real power comes from uniting with others, not subordinating them.

The false self fears poverty, so it desires wealth, not realizing that real wealth comes from love and loving relationships.

The false self fears obscurity, so it desires recognition, not realizing that all the recognition in the world will not make it feel seen or erase the sense of lack it feels.

The false self fears death, so it desires to live on in monuments, not realizing that it never did exist and that what is real is eternal.

The false self fears aging, so it desires the fountain of youth, not realizing that it is not the body.

The false self fears not knowing, so it desires knowledge, not realizing that knowledge without wisdom is folly.

The false self fears imprisonment, so it desires to imprison those it perceives as enemies, not realizing that the real enemy is within.

The false self fears dependence, so it desires individuality and separation, not realizing that Oneness and interdependence is the nature of life and the individual's own salvation.

The false self fears being unloved and alone, so it desires love from others, not realizing that love is not something you get from others, but what you experience when you give love *to* others.

The false self is not wise enough to recognize these truths. It knows nothing of truth, only the opposite of truth. The false self is the purveyor of untruth. That is what it is. It is, after all, the *false* self and named that for a reason. It is not only an imposter and unreal, but its perceptions are false and its desires therefore misguided.

This is not to say there is anything wrong with the ego's desires. It is natural to have an ego and to have such desires. There is also nothing wrong with pursuing these desires. Doing so provides experiences and the many lessons that come with having those experiences, and ultimately the truth about egoic desires is discovered. It just would be a mistake to assume that getting what the ego wants is the purpose of your life or of life in general. That is much too shortsighted a view and overlooks a much grander purpose.

What is that purpose? The overarching purpose is to return to the Father by reclaiming your sonship, by recognizing your own inner divinity. Aside from that, each of you has a purpose for choosing to be on earth at this time in your particular body-mind. You came here for a reason. That reason is for the most part unknown to you, as it is meant to be, for your purpose is, in a sense, to discover your purpose, which happens in the course of living your life.

Life reveals your purpose to you in a variety of ways. It brings you certain experiences, people, and opportunities, and it closes the door on others. The Father has a design for your life, and it is unveiled little by little, moment by moment. The design unfolds each day as it is meant to.

In the midst of this unfolding design, you make choices about the life that is being given to you. You choose the specifics and you choose your attitude and responses, but you do not choose the stage upon which your life is set. Although your life is by no means scripted or predetermined, it is circumscribed, steered, shaped, and sometimes determined by particular events that you are meant to experience.

A higher plan is in effect in people's lives, whether they are aware of that or not. To the extent that they are aware of that plan or are willing to see that there is one, they are more likely to align with it and be fulfilled by it. On the other hand, to the extent that they see the purpose of their life as getting what they want and they judge the value and rightness of their life by how successfully they manage to do that, they will suffer.

Although you have been given free will for a reason, life is not here to support your personal will, but to fulfill a greater plan in which your individual will plays only a small part. The more your individual will is aligned with the higher will, the happier you will be. When your will is identical to Thy will, you thrive and find the deepest contentment and peace.

You know that you are aligned with Thy will when you feel the peace, contentment, joy, and love of your inner divinity. This is what I am calling the Son, or the true self. The Father *in you* is the Son.

The Son knows the way, while the false self does not. The false self doesn't even recognize that there is a way, much less know the way. But the Son does. This divine spark is given to you so that you don't lose your way in life, so that you will fulfill your destiny, your designated purpose.

What I am saying about life is not a religious fairytale, told to appease you within a sorrowful and hopelessly desolate world, but the absolute truth about life. Too many have discarded the truth hidden in religious teachings because they could not accept other aspects of those teachings. But the truth about life is beyond any belief system or religion and can be readily observed and experienced easily enough for those who have eyes to see.

The truth is that your life is divinely designed and divinely guided moment to moment by loving forces whose sole purpose is to serve you. Many of you are able to feel or even communicate with these forces, so for you, this truth is self-evident. But for those who are not aware of their presence, the first step is to *believe* that these guiding forces exist. Once you believe this, you will begin to experience their presence. Belief in their existence opens the door for greater awareness of them and for receiving even more assistance from them.

What you believe determines what you experience. This is how that works: Spiritual forces respect your free will, so they allow you to make choices and experience the results of those choices. If you choose to believe that nothing exists beyond the physical, then you won't notice anything more subtle than your five senses. Even if, on occasion, you do notice something, you will discount and overlook it, thereby reinforcing your belief that spiritual forces don't exist. On the other hand, if you believe that spiritual forces exist, then that belief invites them to more actively assist you. Because you believe you are being guided, you are likely to notice instances when that is the case, thereby confirming your belief—and the truth.

Guiding forces do assist you to some extent even if you do not believe in them because such forces are intrinsic and essential to human evolution. However, they will participate in your life much more fully if you invite them to. That participation can only be beneficial because their nature is goodness and their purpose is to serve humankind. It is not within them to harm or mislead you. The closer you are to these loving forces, the more they are able to protect you from those whose intentions are to interfere with your happiness and life plan, since such forces do exist as well.

The knowledge that life is this benevolent can't help but open your heart. Those who have a connection with other dimensions and levels of their being naturally feel love: for life, for God, for creation, call it what you will. When you are in touch with the truth about life, you feel happy, loving, and at peace. Feeling this way is your birthright! This is how you are meant to feel and how you *can* feel.

Love is the natural outcome of knowing the truth and not being taken in by the fear and lies of the false self. When you surrender the false self, you fall into the truth, into the love that is behind all creation, which happens to also be within *you*. The greatest fulfillment is feeling this love, because love is the greatest truth about life. Love is God, the force behind creation, your very being, and what upholds your very existence. Love created all that is and love is what sustains it.

Two thousand years ago, I came to redeem the world through love: to right any misunderstandings, teach love, and proclaim the truth, which is that this is a loving universe and each of you is the beloved Son of a caring and forgiving Father.

Punishment and vengefulness have never been the intent behind any difficulty you experience. God is love and has nothing but love for creation. Within creation is free will, and the gift of free will is sometimes a curse, as you are free to choose to believe thoughts that cause you to suffer, limit yourself, and harm others. That you choose to believe those thoughts is not the intent of God, but chosen freely by you.

You could argue that God created the ego and therefore suffering, but you would be forgetting that *you* are God incarnate as the Son, that you, as God and through your soul, willingly chose to become human and to experience all that comes with that, including having an ego.

Because people have forgotten that they have chosen this, at times they feel victimized by the hardships of this world and by the emotions, conflict, and problems created by their own egos. They blame God for their pain without realizing that most of it is self-generated and perpetuated by an ego that does not know how to love.

God challenges Himself/Herself by creating a world such as yours with both a positive and negative pole. This means that there are beings who are oriented toward love (the positive pole) and those who are oriented toward fear and power (the negative pole, or the opposite of love).

Beings who are oriented toward fear and power or who themselves have an ego are responsible for creating and sustaining the ego in humanity. And God allows that to be as it is. God allows for His/Her creations to create in ways that might cause suffering, all the while knowing that this will result in learning and better choices. Eventually, everyone relinquishes the negative pole and returns home to Love.

Having an ego makes it possible to experience negativity and, by contrast, to appreciate the positive pole: love. Moreover, the negative pole brings experiences that you/God would never otherwise have and growth that you/God would never otherwise have. Yes, God grows or, more accurately, God's creations grow and evolve, and God is enriched by that.

To return to the subject of surrender, it may be necessary to surrender at least some of your ego's desires at the feet of Thy will. Surrendering all of these desires is never necessary, only the ones that might interfere with the accomplishment of Thy will. If you are unwilling to surrender those or if you are unaware of the need to surrender them, then you are likely to suffer, as Thy will, will be done. The conflict between the small will and the greater will and the unwillingness to surrender the small will to divine will is one of the primary causes of human suffering.

The ego is sure that what it wants is what it needs, and that misunderstanding causes so much suffering. Attachment to what the ego wants is strengthened by the belief that those desires are important and meaningful, when they aren't.

You cannot name an egoic desire that is actually important and meaningful. Any desire that is important and meaningful does not come from the ego but from your divinity, your true self. That is how you know whether a desire is important or not: Where does it come from?

It is possible to tell where a desire comes from by paying close attention to the experience of that desire. Take the desire "I want more money." When you let yourself experience wanting more money, what does that feel like in your body and energy? It feels tight and contracted, right? Now, let yourself feel the desire "I want more love." Even that feels contracted. The problem is "I want."

Anything that follows those two words, "I want," is bound to create a sense of contraction, even "I want love, peace, and joy." Even higher desires such as these feel contracted when expressed as a thought with "I" as the subject. This is because they are being expressed by the "I," or false self, which inherently feels empty and lacking.

The false self wants something because it perceives itself as not having it, as lacking it and therefore needing it. The truth, however, is that you do not lack anything you need, especially love, peace, and joy, because these are qualities of your essential nature and cannot *not* be already here.

It is impossible to lack love, peace, or joy, so "I want more love, peace, and joy" is a statement that is not aligned with the reality that love, peace, and joy are already here. When you think or believe something that is not aligned with reality, you feel contracted, and rightfully so! The contraction or tension in your body lets you know that what you are thinking is not true.

An important and meaningful desire, on the other hand, is simply *felt*. You might put that desire into words, but it doesn't initially appear as a thought. As soon as you put it into words, those words make you feel as if something is missing. If you don't put it into words but just feel that desire and allow it to move you as it will, then you will be expressing divine will.

Thy will is not experienced as the thought "I want," but as a feeling, urge, inspiration, or drive that moves you in a particular direction. Everyone has felt this and does feel this many times a day. You are naturally moved throughout your day by something that is alive in you and motivating you to sustain yourself and unfold your life plan. This mysterious something is Thy will, as expressed through the Son, the Divine in you.

This means that if you surrender "I want," you won't lose anything but a sense of lack and a possible misdirection of your energy. In its place, something else arises, which moves you to take actions or take a rest, as necessary. You can trust this inner force to live your life. It is all that ever has lived your life, although this innate motivation so often gets coopted by the ego.

The more you let go of "I want," the more you make room for something else to move you, and that something is very wise, very kind, and knows exactly what you need to be happy and fulfilled. What it wants *is* really what you need. This motivating force is love.

Chapter 5

Surrendering Knowing

Surrendering knowing is not about surrendering actual knowledge but surrendering untruths and the pretense of actual knowledge. What makes this especially challenging is that people often don't realize they are holding onto untruths or pretending to know. The egoic mind is very tricky!

Built into your thoughts is the sense that they are true, so why would you question them? That is the problem. People generally don't question their thoughts because they assume their thoughts are true or, at the very least, that those thoughts are their own real opinions about life and, therefore, valuable and at least personally true.

Knowledge is a good thing. No one would argue that. Knowing how to get from your home to where you work is essential. Knowing what day it is, what words to use to describe things, how to read, how to do math, how to test a hypothesis—this knowledge is necessary and extremely useful.

The part of your brain that learns, retains knowledge, and evaluates and applies knowledge is exactly what is needed to see that the thoughts that come into your mind do not pass the intelligence test. You have a mind that learns and processes knowledge, and you have the thoughts that come into your mind—the egoic mind. These are two very different kinds of thinking: one is intelligent and the other is essentially programming.

If you had a computerized voice that was programmed with some information, rules, and general advice, you would have something close to the egoic mind, with one very important difference: The egoic mind is petty, unkind, judgmental, bossy, critical, and generally dissatisfied. If this does not describe your egoic mind, then you are one of the few fortunate souls who was gifted with a computerized inner voice that is not also a complainer.

Surrendering Knowing

Progress along the spiritual path often neutralizes some of the negativity of one's thoughts, but rarely does the egoic mind disappear completely. In all likelihood, the voice in your head is there to stay and must be dealt with.

The first step in dealing with the egoic mind is getting to know it: What are the thoughts that run through your mind? What are the most common ones? Write them down. That way, you can examine them more objectively.

The second step is to do just that—question your thoughts: Are they true? Are they useful? Do you need them? How do they affect you? Do you like how you are being affected by them? If not, what can you do about that?

The third step is to see that you have some power in relation to your thoughts. They are, after all, yours, so you can do with them what you choose. You can believe them and act on them *or not*. You can evaluate the possible consequences of acting on them before you do and choose otherwise if you don't want those consequences.

Life is a great mystery and so are human beings. There are many more questions than answers. You can know lots of things and lots of facts and still not know what life is all about, what your life is about, why things are the way they are, what's going to happen, why people behave the way they do or did, why things happened the way they did, and on and on. There are many more things that you don't know and never will know than you do. It's important to realize and admit this.

This is where the false self falls down: It does not admit what it doesn't know. Instead, it pretends to know things that can never be known as well as things that may be known at some point but aren't known yet. If you met someone who did this, you would call that person a pathological liar, which is someone who makes up things that aren't true and tries to pass them off on others as if they were true. That is a description of your egoic mind.

Do you need these thoughts? This is a very good question. Take a look and answer this for yourself. You certainly don't need any thoughts that don't actually have the answer to something but pretend to. Spotting such thoughts isn't actually that hard. You just have to stop a moment and ask yourself, "Do I really know that?" You may be quite surprised at how often the answer is no.

Surrendering Knowing

This is how you discover the truth about your thoughts. You have to ask yourself some questions. They are very simple questions, but ones that most people don't ever think to ask themselves. If you even suggest to others that they question their thoughts, most will look at you funny, as if there's something wrong with you.

The programming does not want to be questioned. It is not meant to be uncovered. And yet the truth eventually comes out at some point in a person's evolution. It is time now in humanity's evolution for the truth to come out, which is why there are more and more teachings like this one being made available.

The world can no longer withstand the ego's domination. The ego must be made subordinate, and love must take its place. But because you have free will, you have to do the work yourself of seeing this and freeing yourself from your own ego. Those of us assisting humanity in this transformation can only point out the truth.

Here are some common examples of the mind pretending to know when it doesn't:

You think you know what someone thinks about you.

You think you know how someone feels about you.

You think you know how someone feels about something.

You think you know why something happened or why someone did what he or she did.

You think you know what someone else is going to do.

You think you know what you are going to do.

You think you know what someone else should do.

You think you know what you should do.

You think you know what will make someone happy.

You think you know what will make you happy.

You think you will like or not like someone (as if you ever feel just one way about someone).

You think you know how some experience will feel.

You think you know how you will feel in the future.

You think you know what's going to happen in the world.

You think you know what is happening in the world.

You think you know the solution to what's happening in the world.

You think you know what your life is going to look like tomorrow.

You think you know what you are going to do tomorrow.

You think you know what you are going to do in the next few hours.

You think...

"I think..." Watch those two words, please, as they point to speculation on the part of the mind, a mere idea that is often based on very little information or knowledge. Often such thoughts have no basis in reality whatsoever. The mind just likes to think, so it thinks thoughts. It comes up with ideas pretty much out of the blue. Notice how much of your conversations with others are based on opinions and theories about anything and everything.

This is what the mind does. It produces thoughts, opinions, judgments, and evaluations, among other things. These are not the objective evaluations and conclusions that your rational mind is capable of, but a horse of a completely different color. This is not intelligence functioning, but programming. Pure and simple. Watch the mind. See for yourself.

Seeing the truth can be quite humbling—and extremely freeing. You become free of the need to have an opinion about everything, to know about all of the things that you never could know about anyway. What a relief it is to not have to know everything! And to not *need* to know. The false self feels a need to know everything, even when it can't, while the true self simply knows what it needs to know when it needs to know it, without desiring anything more than that.

Another benefit of disengaging from the mind's pretend knowings is that your mental energy is freed up for other activities, perhaps for learning or for some other practical or fun application of the mind. Since you can only be involved in one kind of mental activity at a time, what will it be: the idle speculation of the egoic mind, including all the thoughts about yourself, or more intellectual pursuits such as questioning your thoughts, investigating the more subtle realms, reading, learning, or creating something?

One of the most wonderful gifts you have been given is a mind that can explore, imagine, create, and learn. The being that you are is naturally curious and fascinated by life and loves to learn. Such enjoyable mental activities can replace the useless ruminations, fantasies, and speculations of the mind.

When you are spending less time mentally spinning your wheels and dealing with the emotions generated by that, you will have more time for more fun, fulfilling, and meaningful activities, including just being. Furthermore, a quieter mind means you will be able to tune in to the spiritual Heart and its guidance more easily.

When you stop listening to the mind and begin listening more deeply to something much subtler than the mind, your life will change. Then it will be possible for you to see how truly good life is, how supportive and trustworthy it is. Your thoughts were what was creating any harshness, anxiety, fear, distrust, stress, and dissatisfaction you felt. Once you stop creating a negative internal climate by listening to your thoughts, then all that is left is love, wonder, awe, gratitude and joy—the truth about life. When life is stripped of the ego's perceptions and emotions and experienced through different eyes, life is seen more truly. Love is all around for those who have eyes to see it.

When you see from the eyes of love, you see love. When you see from the ego's eyes, you see life as the ego sees it. Whatever lens you look from is what you see and what you experience. If you want to change your life, change the lens through which you look. All real change and transformation is the result of such a change of lens.

All that has ever kept you from your true self are your false ideas. These ideas are everything you think you know about yourself and everything else. With every false idea that you surrender, you are transformed, and the lens through which you look becomes clearer. In this way, you become who you are meant to be: your true self.

The process of becoming clearer—or empty, as the Buddhists say—is to recognize how much you do not know, notice how attached your ego is to pretending to know, and offer this attachment and all misunderstandings and false ideas to the Father. Give them to Him. Lay them at His feet. Imagining yourself doing this is a very powerful act of clearing. This act strengthens your intention to become free of such useless thoughts and calls forth spiritual forces to help you with this.

To enter the Father's palace, you have to surrender your attachment to knowing, not to real knowledge, but attachment to the ego's false beliefs and assumptions, which create and maintain the false self. To surrender this, you have to be willing to not know, which the ego is not. What *is* willing to not know is the true self.

This surrender may seem difficult, but all it takes is a *willingness* to surrender and a *willingness* to not know. This willingness will naturally take you to surrender. Your intention is powerful! It is an important ingredient in the process of surrendering the false self. You don't need to know how to surrender; you only need to be willing to, and the *how* is taken care of.

Are you willing? Are you willing to be stripped bare of all thoughts about yourself, the past, the future, what you think you know, and what you'd like to know? What would that be like? Who would you be? You would lose a lot of what seems to make you who you are, but you would not be losing anything that is real, and what you would gain is your true self.

How can I describe your true self to you? There are no words, but it is closer to you than your breath. The true self is known only through experience, and the more experiences you have of it, the deeper those experiences become and the more real the reality of the true self becomes. There is no end to the depths of this self. Are you willing to experience it and stay in that experience for as long as it takes to get to know your true self? Now, that is true knowing!

Stop a moment and feel what it is like to be in this moment, stripped of all knowing. What remains? What is that? Consciousness? Existence? You exist. You are conscious. You exist *as* consciousness, and that is all! That is all you really know. In not needing to know anything more than that, lies peace. You have come Home. You can just be. Finally, there is no need to grasp after more, to know more. What you know is enough. Existence is enough.

Surrendering Knowing

And then... you find yourself being moved by some knowing that arises from deep within you. Without warning or knowing why, suddenly you feel called to act, and you answer that call. You don't need to know anything more. Answering that call is natural, spontaneous, and automatic, except sometimes you stop yourself—your thoughts stop you.

The call sometimes comes in the form of an idea that pops into your mind, but it is unlike the usual thoughts. It has been described as a light bulb going on or an "aha!" because that is what an idea from the Father feels like. It feels expansive, good, and true. When the call lands in the body, it is often described as an intuition or a download.

You are given instructions for this life, which are delivered little by little, moment to moment, as you need them. These instructions are usually very sparse; nothing is given that you don't immediately need. They are more like pointers or clues for you to follow in your own way.

These pointers are very different from the mind's instructions, which are spelled out specifically and handed out continually. If only those thoughts were wise! But the Father wants *you*, the Son, the unique and beloved individual that He created and infused with His spirit, to choose the specifics, not your ego. The Father gave you free will so that you could fill in the specifics as you will. The Father guides you only generally and then steps back to enjoy what you choose to create *with* Him.

The Father's instructions do not feel at all like the demands and to-do lists of the egoic mind but more like reminders, nudges, encouragement, inspiration, motivation, and excitement about doing something or taking on something. In that way, they are not like instructions at all. They offer no long-term plan or reasons why or details, except what you might receive moment to moment, and there is no requirement that you fulfill these instructions, although doing so feels right and brings you joy.

The Father's instructions are a gift, an ongoing guiding Presence that is designed to take care of you, make you happy, and fulfill you in this lifetime. You can trust the knowings from your spiritual Heart to do that. They are what unfolds life and always has, alongside the dictates of your mind.

Now that you know that you need only the Father's instructions, you can disregard the voice in your head, the imposter who poses as the captain. You never needed that voice, but you had to discover that for yourself. And you have had to discover for yourself that still, small voice. And now, moment to moment, it is up to you to choose that quiet, unimposing voice over the ego's noisy, imperious one.

There has always been a plan, and you have always been guided to fulfill it through that still, small voice. That voice is rarely a voice, and yet everyone knows what is meant when it is described this way, because it is closer to you than anything else. It is, in essence, your own voice calling you Home.

Chapter 6

Surrendering to Love in Relationships

I have been speaking about surrendering thoughts in exchange for experiencing the love that is your true nature. This chapter will explore what it means to share this love with others through relationship. It is one thing to drop into the unconditional love of your true nature and quite another to be able to bring that love into your relationships, where one is so often challenged by another's conditioning and ego as well as one's own.

What I mean by conditioning is the preferences, personality traits, beliefs, images, fantasies, desires, fears, psychological issues, and habit patterns that cause people to behave reflexively and automatically in the ways they generally do. The false self is the sum total of this conditioning plus the ego. The true self is what you are beyond the ego and all of this conditioning, and it is what is capable of love.

Conditioning is responsible for all the ways people are different from each other. In addition to the ego, these differences are what cause problems in relationships. In any of your relationships, you are going to have to relate to the other person's ego and conditioning, and that's where relationships run into trouble. The true selves don't have a problem with each other; after all, they are in essence the same!

Because most people relate to other people's egos and conditioning from their own ego and conditioning, most relationships are an experience of one ego relating to another and one set of conditioning battling with another. On that level, love doesn't stand a chance. Egos want to get their way and be right more than they want love. They will fight to the death of the relationship, and often do.

The only chance that love has is if two people are able to experience their own true self and that of the other at least some of the time. Fortunately, experiencing your true self is not only *not* impossible, but inevitable if love is given half a chance. The true self in each person *is* love and lives for love, so the true selves of each are always pulling the person toward love. Love is a very powerful force in people's lives, and the drive for love motivates people to keep trying to find the love that they know in their heart is possible. Love is possible, and something inside you knows this and, against all odds (the ego), keeps trying to get it right.

The ego is the enemy of love. It fears love, although it needs other people's love to feel good about itself and to feel safe. And yet, relationships feel quite unsafe and challenging to the ego because of its lack of control over the other person and the potential hurt involved in relationships. Love presents quite a dilemma to the ego!

Because the ego is incompatible with love, a relationship will be only as strong and loving as both people's ability to surrender their own egos. The surrender I am talking about is not a sacrificing, or subjugation, of one person in deference to the other's needs and ego, which often happens in relationship, but the recognition by both that mutual happiness is possible only when both are willing to put love and the relationship first and sort out their differences from that vantage point. *Both* must be willing to surrender their egos and conditioning for a higher cause—for love and for the relationship.

In the face of a conflict, which is inevitably about differences in conditioning, often one person has to surrender his or her ego's position first before the other person will. As in a war, when one side puts down its weapons, the other side will too. Once that is done, peace—love—is possible, and a mutually agreed upon solution to those differences can be found from the vantage point of the true selves.

Most of the time, however, the battle around conditioning is a personal one and is best if it remains a personal one. What I mean by this is that the battle is *within* you and doesn't have to involve the other person. It is your personal battle with your own conditioning and ego, which demands that your partner be more like you or comply with your likes, dislikes, expectations, fantasies, and desires. The conditioning itself isn't necessarily a problem, but your ego makes it a problem by demanding that others change to please you, to meet your needs, to match your expectations, desires, fantasies, and images.

Your conditioning doesn't have to become a problem for the relationship. If you don't like something about your partner, is that your problem, your partner's problem, or both? Most of the time, it is simply your problem, but you make it your partner's problem and, consequently, something the relationship has to deal with. *Your* problem—some unmet expectation or desire or your dislike of something—becomes a problem in the relationship.

Many issues could be solved quite easily if people simply recognized the difference between their personal issue with someone and a real problem that needs the other person's attention. Most problems in relationship are caused simply by one person not liking something about the other: one person's conditioning bumping up against the other's. This is always going to happen. There will always be differences.

The solution is not to try to eliminate these differences by changing the other person, which is what the ego naturally tries to do, but by changing your relationship to your own conditioning. Realizing that your expectations, desires, fantasies, and preferences are just your conditioning and that they are what cause you to suffer, not your partner, makes it possible to relate to that conditioning differently, to take responsibility for it and to hold it more lightly and not put it above love and the relationship. Conditioning and one's desires are not more important than love and relationship. If you give your conditioning and desires more importance than love, as the ego does, then love won't thrive within your relationship. Your demands, needs, expectations, judgments, and desires will kill the relationship.

The ego views the differences that are produced by conditioning suspiciously. It sees those who are different as wrong, bad, or inferior—which would be everybody! The ego feels justified by a sense of self-righteousness in trying to change or reform others. The ego's favorite tools of "reform," which are really ways of trying to manipulate others to get its way, are judgment, criticism, anger, bullying, threats, and withdrawal or withholding. The ego's motto in relationships is: "My way or the highway."

Such tactics are extremely damaging to relationships and have no place in relationships. Love cannot survive in such an unfriendly climate. But the ego would rather have its way than have love. Many endure or perpetuate such a hostile atmosphere and wonder why they don't feel love for their partner. But you can't expect love and judgment or other forms of unkindness to coexist. That is expecting too much.

It is also *accepting* too much. Judgment and other forms of unkindness are unacceptable in relationship. If you are participating in unkindness or allowing unkindness to flourish in your relationship, then you are accepting too much. You are not holding your relationship to a high enough standard. By all means accept differences, but do not accept judgment or unkindness, and don't contribute to it yourself.

If judgment and other unkind words or acts are going on in your relationship, then it is only a matter of time before the relationship ends or is declared "loveless." Judgment, criticism, anger, blame, and unkindness must be surrendered to love, or love will die.

Under those conditions love will die because you will no longer trust or feel safe with each other. Love requires trust and safety, because without these, you cannot relax. If you can't relax with your partner, you won't be able to experience your true self and therefore love. You will remain on guard, and what remains on guard is the ego. If, in your relationship, trust has been eroded, experiencing your partner from anything other than the ego will be difficult.

Relaxation and trust allow you to move out of the fearful world of the ego into the peace and love of the true self. For becoming established in a state of relaxation, safety, and peace, meditation is extremely helpful. Meditation is the bridge between the false self's world and the true self's. The more you travel this bridge in meditation, the easier it will be to travel it in the midst of your busy life and in the presence of any conflict in your relationship. Without this ability to move out of the ego and the willingness to relinquish the ego's weapons, resolving conflicts and differences in your relationships will continue to be very challenging.

The only solution to your ego (which is the only ego you are responsible for) is to find that which lies within you that does not judge but accepts differences and allows others to be as they are. The true self loves others as they are and lets them be as they are. The true self accepts the partner's differences, quirks, and imperfections, just as you would hope your partner would do for you. The true self lives and lets live, as long as the partner's behavior is not abusive or destructive, in which case your true self would have you leave the relationship.

Wouldn't it be easy to love someone who let you be as you are, who accepted you just the way you are, without trying to change you or even wanting you to be different? Are you willing to give the same acceptance and freedom to your partner? Are you willing to allow your partner to live his or her life as he or she sees fit and make his or her mistakes and learn from them? Isn't that also the freedom you want and need? This is love. This is the acceptance that every human being craves and deserves. When people accept each other and give each other the freedom to be as they are and as they choose to be, love flows between them.

If something your partner is doing grates against your conditioning or disappoints you, then you need to look at your conditioning and surrender that rather than try to change the other person's conditioning. It is not your job to change other people; it is your job to love them.

Often surrender (love) requires letting go of a desire or a fantasy: the desire for your partner to be better looking, richer, stronger, more intelligent, younger, more masculine, more feminine, thinner, more voluptuous, more muscular, neater, more organized, more responsible, more exciting, more adventuresome.... These are some of the things the ego values and desires, many of which show up in its fantasies.

These desires are quite superficial but important to the ego. All egos have such desires. Any desire you have for these things is not unique—or meaningful. Such desires are just your programming, how you have been conditioned to think and feel. They have nothing to do with your capacity to love someone, nor are they indicators of people you are best suited to be with.

Many hold their desires for their partner to be different secretly, without telling their partner of their dissatisfaction. Although that is preferable to sharing your dissatisfactions with your partner, keeping them to yourself is not the same as surrendering them. Unless you actually surrender your desires for your partner to be different, they are likely to interfere with your ability to love your partner.

Desires, such as the ego has, lead to a sense of disappointment and dissatisfaction and often to withdrawal or withholding of love. "If only he (or she) were more..., then I would be so in love!" The bad news (the reality) is that your partner will never become what you want him or her to be. But the good news is that your partner doesn't have to for you to have a loving relationship. You only have to see that your desires are no reason to withhold your love from your partner.

When you don't withhold your love, you feel love and you feel happy. That is the magic of love: It resides in you, and you feel it when you are willing to give it. The ego holds love back, as if love were a bargaining chip: "I'll love you if...." But doing that only makes you the loser. You lose the opportunity to feel love. You are the one who controls how much love you feel in a relationship: When you love, you feel love. It is a choice to love and a choice to withhold it, although often an unconscious one.

Become conscious of the ways you may be withholding love from your partner because your ego finds him or her unworthy of it or because, on some level, you feel you gain something by withholding love: Power? Control? Superiority? Safety? What is it you think you gain in holding back your love, in not jumping into your relationship with both feet? Are you angry at your partner for not doing or being something you want him or her to be, and are you withholding love to punish your partner or to try to get your partner to do what you want?

The person in front of you is the person that life has given you to love. You chose this person out of all the people that life presented you with. You can choose to give that person love or try to find another. But to choose to stay with someone and not love him or her doesn't make much sense, except perhaps to the ego, which often stays in a loveless relationship out of fear or a desire for security.

So then the question becomes, "How do I surrender my desires for my partner to be different?" If this sounds difficult, that is only because the ego believes that its desires are really important and that it *needs* the partner to fit a certain image or fantasy in order to be happy—which is true of the ego, but not of the true self, which is what loves. To love, you have to set the ego's perceptions aside and look through different eyes, the eyes of something that *does* know how to love. You surrender the ego's perceptions for love, in order *to* love.

To the ego, surrendering desires sounds difficult (and why would it want to?), but doing this is not actually difficult. All that needs to be surrendered are thoughts. Desires, fantasies, and everything else the ego holds dear are just ideas. How difficult is it to let go of an idea? Don't you do this all the time? Thoughts arise, desires arise, and you often disregard them. You know how to do this. You already practice this daily with some thoughts.

Desires are essentially the thought "I want." If a desire has been thought about a lot, it also has a feeling component, but it stems from a thought. Is it so difficult to disregard that thought? It is difficult if you aren't aware of that thought. If you aren't aware that you are withholding love because of a desire, then you first have to become conscious of that desire and the importance you have given it. Then, once you see how empty and false that desire is, how it undermines love, and how unimportant it is in relation to the true goal, which is love, then surrendering that desire becomes easier.

Stories and images of the partner may also need to be surrendered, not only desires. With any desire, there is probably a story you tell yourself or an image you hold of your partner. For instance, if you wish your partner were physically stronger and more muscular, you might tell yourself a story something like this: "He's weak, not masculine, not sexy, so I don't feel attracted to him." And then you have a mental image that goes along with that of him being weak and unattractive. You see him a certain way in your mind's eye, which can be quite different than reality, because the mind distorts and leaves out much of reality.

When you look at him, you overlay that story and image onto him and see him through that lens. You don't actually see him, the whole of him. You aren't seeing what you love about him and what you *are* attracted to. You aren't seeing his good qualities, only what you think is lacking. You are focusing only on the negatives, which is what the ego does.

If you focus on this story and image long enough over time and talk to your friends about it, then this becomes your experience of your partner—your reality—and you begin to relate to your partner differently than if you didn't have that story and image. You create the experience of "I'm not attracted to my partner. I'm not in love with him."

That unimportant fact about him, that he isn't muscular, has been made overly important (by the ego) and now overshadows other things that are true about him and that do matter in the realm of love, canceling out your feelings of love.

There are four people in every relationship: the two real people and their internal images of each other. When both people have positive images of each other, they feel good about each other. Love flows. On the other hand, when one or both are holding negative images, there is usually trouble. Happy couples have consistently positive images of each other, at least consistent enough to sustain love, while unhappy couples have problematic images of each other. These images are in large part created and maintained by thoughts.

What you focus on in your thoughts about your partner either creates love or destroys love. You are very powerful that way. Your thoughts create an internal image of your partner, which produces feelings about your partner, which manifests as behavior toward your partner. Your inner reality becomes "your truth," and that affects the relationship.

If you don't want the reality that your thoughts, stories, and images create, then don't empower those thoughts with your attention. Instead, turn your attention onto what you love and are grateful for about your partner. Talk to your friends about that, if you must say anything, and be sure to express what you are grateful for to your partner.

It is easy to find fault! It is the easiest thing in the world. But if you focus on your partner's faults, you will fall out of love with your partner. If you focus on your partner's good qualities, you will stay in love with your partner. Your attention is that powerful. You create love and you destroy it.

So love requires surrendering not only your desires for your partner to be different, but also your negative stories and images of your partner. As with all surrender, all you really need is the *willingness* to surrender, and the Father does the rest. So give the ego's desires, negative stories, and images to the Father. Lay them at His feet, and He will release you from them. This giving them to the Father involves having an intention for His help and then not touching these thoughts when they arise, both of which take no time or effort whatsoever.

When these destructive desires and negative stories and images arise in your mind, notice them, recognize that they belong to the ego, and lay them at the Father's feet. Do not touch them. You don't need to have your ego's desires met to be happy or to feel love. And you don't need to destroy your relationship with a story or an image.

Then once your egoic desires and negative stories and images have been surrendered, if there remains a flame of love between you and your partner that can be fanned, it is up to you to do that. Sometimes people find that they aren't actually a match for or in love with their partner. Perhaps the love that was once there has been irretrievably destroyed or maybe it was never there to begin with.

When a relationship is founded on the things the ego values, there often isn't enough to sustain the relationship long term. Many people fall in love with an idea or image of someone, and when that person fails to live up to that, they cling to the hope that he or she will somehow become that image, or they continue to try to manipulate that person to fit that image. When false hope and manipulation, both tactics of the ego, are given up, two people might not be left with much on which to base a relationship. On the other hand, they might be left with a greater possibility for love than ever.

Love is a great mystery! What is that force that brings two people together? Sometimes it is mere physical attraction: Each person's internal images of the perfect partner are personified in each other, so they fall in love. But sometimes there is something much more than that present—true love—that gives meaning, purpose, and longevity to a relationship. You love the person's soul—who he or she *really* is, on a deep level. You love that person's *being*, and you can't imagine life without him or her. You are partners in life and supports for each other. What a blessing it is to find such a love!

Even those strong matches need to be nourished with positive thoughts and gratitude day by day, or the relationship may wither. Even in the best of relationships, you have to watch your thoughts! At any time, the ego's need to be right can rear its ugly head, and before you know it, you have traded being right for being loving.

People think they need their desires, fantasies, and expectations to be met to be happy and to be in love, but they don't! They place the responsibility for their happiness on someone else, on conditions outside themselves: "I will be happy when he (or she)...." Instead of realizing that their happiness is their responsibility and in their own hands, they think it is someone else's responsibility and in someone else's hands.

The ego's strategy for happiness is to try to get other people to behave a certain way, look a certain way, or do things a certain way. "If only I could get the world to comply with my desires, I would be happy, and *then* I will be loving." That is the ego's excuse for not being happy or loving *now*.

But there is no excuse for not being happy and not being loving now. It is your responsibility to be happy and to be loving, and this is something in life you *can* control. You can't control other people or most circumstances, but you can control your internal state. *You* make *you* happy, and only you can.

The beauty of this is that when you are happy and not making demands on others for your happiness, others find you irresistibly lovable. A happy and loving internal state creates a happy and loving external reality. You get what you want—happiness and love—by *being* what you want the other person to be: happy and loving.

If you want love in your life, you have to give love. There is no way around it! It is a natural law: Love attracts more of the same. Of course, the opposite is true: Judgment and unkindness attract judgment and unkindness. If you don't want judgment and unkindness in your relationships, then eliminate them within yourself.

The ego blames others for its unhappiness, when, in fact, it creates its own unhappiness. The ego creates a negative internal state. Then instead of taking responsibility for that, it blames others: "You made me angry! If it weren't for you, I'd be happy. You are the cause of all my problems. You don't love me enough." The truth is that your thoughts made you angry. If it weren't for your thoughts, you'd be happy. Your thoughts are the cause of all your problems. Your ego doesn't love others enough.

Your partner is not responsible for making you happy. Blaming others keeps you from realizing that you have the power to love and make yourself happy. Blaming also hurts others unnecessarily. Of course, that is the ego's intent. It is the ego's way of asserting its superiority and power. Blaming, like judging, has no place in relationships. Besides, blame is never true. It leaves out too much of the story.

Having said all this, I don't mean to imply that you can be happy and in love with just anyone. That is too much to expect. Although one's attitude makes a tremendous difference in how you experience any relationship you are in, you aren't meant to be with just anyone. The true love I am speaking about comes rarely in one's life. It takes a special combination of people, and those two people have to continue to nurture that gift of love.

The point I am making in this chapter is that to make the most of any relationship, the ego must be put aside. Some of those relationships will be passing and some will last, and all serve a purpose in your overall growth and evolution. The degree to which your relationships will be satisfying is the degree to which you are able to set aside your judgments, egoic desires, demands, expectations, and fantasies and simply *be* with the person in front of you, stripped of those, and see him or her through the eyes of love.

When you take responsibility for your own happiness and for all the ways that your conditioning interferes with your happiness, then it is possible to have a truly healthy relationship, one in which two happy people join together out of mutual love and celebration, not out of need or dependency. So what does a healthy relationship between two happy people look like?

❖ You accept that sometimes your partner will judge, get angry, or behave unkindly, but you don't judge, get angry or behave unkindly in retaliation. Instead, you take a few deep breaths, relax, stay present, listen, and respond compassionately. You notice any egoic thoughts, but you surrender them as soon as they arise and keep your attention in the present moment.

❖ When you catch yourself judging, feeling angry, or behaving unkindly, you stop, take a few deep breaths, relax, move out of your mind and emotions, feel your body, experience what you are sensing, have compassion for yourself, forgive yourself, and then say you are sorry and ask your partner for forgiveness. This whole process may take some time.

❖ If you are irritated or upset by something your partner did or didn't do, you look into your own thoughts and see how you created those feelings of irritation or upset by having certain expectations or desires. You remind yourself that your partner's purpose is not to live up to or fulfill your expectations and desires. You surrender your desires or fulfill them yourself or in some other way.

❖ You have fun together. You play together. You laugh together. You find things that give you both pleasure and regularly do those things together. Your love is nourished by dropping into that place of joy together.

❖ You are relaxed and comfortable around each other. You feel like you can just be yourself, without being self-conscious or concerned about how you look or how your partner might judge you.

❖ You have separate interests that you each enjoy apart from each other, and you let each other have those interests. You support each other in doing whatever makes your heart sing. Your partner's cup of tea might not be your cup of tea, but it doesn't have to be. You don't have to be the same. Differences are good and appreciated for the richness they bring to the relationship.

❖ You practice seeing the good in your partner and noticing all the little things he or she does that contribute to your mutual well-being. You notice what you are grateful for about your partner and express your gratitude to your partner regularly for the gift that he or she is to you.

❖ When you disagree with your partner about something practical, like who does what around the house, you calmly state what you would like to have happen, listen to your partner's viewpoint, and then decide together how to resolve the issue so that you are both happy. Trading something for something else might be part of that solution: You do something your partner wants in exchange for your partner doing something you want. Or you do something that your partner doesn't like doing but you don't mind doing in exchange for something you don't like doing but your partner doesn't mind doing.

A chapter about love would not be complete without addressing more fully the importance of forgiveness in relationship. Everyone makes mistakes and is hurtful sometimes, and your partner's mistakes and offenses need to be forgiven, just as yours do.

The ego keeps a tally of every hurt and offense and everything the partner didn't do that he or she was expected to do. When the tally mounts up, the ego exacts its payment through demands, anger, or withholding. This only increases the pain in a relationship, often resulting in the other person retaliating or withholding. Forgiveness sets the scale back to zero so that the relationship can pull itself out of this downward spiral and have a fresh start.

Without forgiveness, resentments and anger pile up and kill love. A lack of forgiveness keeps you focused on the partner's failing or fault or on some incident. It keeps you in the grip of your emotions and at odds with love. Without forgiveness, your ego remains in power in your consciousness, and it will continue to judge the partner and look for further justification for its anger and resentment.

The ego wants to be right, and it wants to see itself as superior. Any failings, faults, or mistakes of the partner are occasions for the ego to puff up, judge, withdraw love, or in some other way punish the partner for those mistakes or failings. The ego clings to this sense of superiority, not caring about the toll it takes on the relationship, the toll it takes on love.

In an attempt to maintain its superiority and sense of being perfect, the ego hides, from itself and others, its own failings and mistakes, denying its own humanity. This is a very unhealthy situation, because compassion and forgiveness cannot easily be accessed from this place of denial and superiority.

Being ego-identified is very lonely and isolating, and to pretend to be above reproach is an impossible burden. The unconscious is bound to sabotage such an ego in some way, as has been frequently demonstrated in cases of well-known preachers being caught with prostitutes. Human fallibility cannot be denied, or it will beg to be proven.

Forgiveness wipes the slate clean so that you can begin again anew, from a place of the true self rather than the ego. Forgiveness is often required before one can move from the ego's prison to the Father's palace. You forgive yourself for allowing the ego to run you, and you forgive your partner for allowing the ego to run him or her.

From there, it is possible to feel compassion for the human condition in which you both find yourselves: You both have egos that can make a mess of your lives and your relationships. These egos are very convincing and seem so powerful at times. Moving beyond the ego's grasp is not easy! You know that, and when you can admit that, you can forgive.

Forgiving your partner for being human allows you to see the Divine in your partner, because forgiveness makes it possible to see through the eyes of the true self. Seeing what you see and experiencing what you experience through these eyes is all you have ever really wanted and what your misguided desires were trying to attain all along. Here love lies, in surrendering everything the ego holds so dear. What a paradox this human experience is, when surrendering is what frees you and delivers everything you have ever wanted.

About the Author

Gina Lake is a nondual spiritual teacher and the author of over twenty books about awakening to one's true nature. She is also a gifted intuitive and channel with a master's degree in Counseling Psychology and over twenty-five years' experience supporting people in their spiritual growth. In 2012, Jesus began dictating books through her. These teachings from Jesus are based on universal truth, not on any religion. Her website offers information about her books and online course, a free ebook, a blog, and audio and video recordings:

www.RadicalHappiness.com

Awakening Now Online Course

This course was created for your awakening. The methods presented are powerful companions on the path to enlightenment and true happiness. In this 100-day inner workout, you'll immerse yourself in materials, practices, guided meditations, and inquiries that will transform your consciousness. And in video webinars, you'll receive transmissions of Christ Consciousness. These transmissions are a direct current of love and healing that will help you break through to a new level of being. By the end of 100 days, you will have developed new habits and ways of being that will result in being more richly alive and present and greater joy and equanimity.

www.RadicalHappiness.com/courses

If you enjoyed this book, you might also enjoy the other two books in this trilogy by Jesus, which is also available in a single volume called The Jesus Trilogy:

Choice and Will: New Teachings from Jesus

Explores the complex, mysterious, and important question of who or what chooses. The question is complex because there is more than one answer. It is mysterious because our nature is mysterious and because the answer may not be what you think. The question is important because our choices shape our reality and determine our experience of it. This book was dictated to Gina Lake by Jesus.

Beliefs, Emotions, and the Creation of Reality: New Teachings from Jesus

Explores the exciting arena of creation: how beliefs determine our internal reality and, consequently, our external reality; how beliefs that stem from the ego and our conditioning distort our perception of ourselves, others, and reality; and specific ways to move beyond these distorted perceptions to a clearer perception of reality and therefore greater happiness and fulfillment. This book was dictated to Gina Lake by Jesus.

www.RadicalHappiness.com

More Books by Gina Lake

Available in paperback, ebook, and audiobook formats.

From Stress to Stillness: Tools for Inner Peace. Most stress is created by how we think about things. *From Stress to Stillness* will help you to examine what you are thinking and change your relationship to your thoughts so that they no longer result in stress. Drawing from the wisdom traditions, psychology, New Thought, and the author's own experience as a spiritual teacher and counselor, *From Stress to Stillness* offers many practices and suggestions that will lead to greater peace and equanimity, even in a busy and stress-filled world.

Ten Teachings for One World is a message from Mother Mary to all her beloved children on earth. The teachings are intended to bring us into closer contact with the peace and love that is our divine nature, which has the ability to transform our hearts and our world. Mother Mary's gentle wisdom will inspire and assist you in awakening to the magnificent being that you are.

Embracing the Now: Finding Peace and Happiness in What Is. The Now—this moment—is the true source of happiness and peace and the key to living a fulfilled and meaningful life. *Embracing the Now* is a collection of essays that can serve as daily reminders of the deepest truths. Full of clear insight and wisdom, *Embracing the Now* explains how the mind keeps us from being in the moment, how to move into the Now and stay there, and what living from the Now is like. It also explains how to overcome stumbling blocks to being in the Now, such as fears, doubts, misunderstandings, judgments, distrust of life, desires, and other conditioned ideas that are behind human suffering.

Radical Happiness: A Guide to Awakening provides the keys to experiencing the happiness that is ever-present and not dependent on circumstances. This happiness doesn't come from getting what you want, but from wanting what is here now. It comes from realizing that who you think you are is not who you really are. This is a radical perspective! *Radical Happiness* describes the nature of the egoic state of consciousness and how it interferes with happiness, what awakening and enlightenment are, and how to live in the world after awakening.

Choosing Love: Moving from Ego to Essence in Relationships. Having a truly meaningful relationship requires choosing love over your conditioning, that is, your ideas, fantasies, desires, images, and beliefs. *Choosing Love* describes how to move beyond conditioning, judgment, anger, romantic illusions, and differences to the experience of love and Oneness with another. It explains how to drop into the core of your Being, where Oneness and love exist, and be with others from there.

In the World but Not of It: New Teachings from Jesus on Embodying the Divine: From the Introduction, by Jesus: "What I have come to teach now is that you can embody love, as I did. You can become Christ within this human life and learn to embody all that is good within you. I came to show you the beauty of your own soul and what is possible as a human. I came to show you that it is possible to be both human and divine, to be love incarnate. You are equally both. You walk with one foot in the world of form and another in the Formless. This mysterious duality within your being is what this book is about." This book is another in a series of books dictated to Gina Lake by Jesus.

Return to Essence: How to Be in the Flow and Fulfill Your Life's Purpose describes how to get into the flow and stay there and how to live life from there. Being in the flow and not being in the flow are two very different states. One is dominated by the ego-driven mind, which is the cause of suffering, while the other is the domain of Essence, the Divine within each of us. You are meant to live in the flow. The flow is the experience of Essence—your true self—as it lives life through you and fulfills its purpose for this life.

Living in the Now: How to Live as the Spiritual Being That You Are. The 99 essays in *Living in the Now* will help you realize your true nature and live as that. They answer many questions raised by the spiritual search and offer wisdom on subjects such as fear, anger, happiness, aging, boredom, desire, patience, faith, forgiveness, acceptance, love, commitment, hope, purpose, meaning, meditation, being present, emotions, trusting life, trusting your Heart, and many other deep subjects. These essays will help you become more conscious, present, happy, loving, grateful, at peace, and fulfilled. Each essay stands on its own and can be used for daily contemplation.

Trusting Life: Overcoming the Fear and Beliefs That Block Peace and Happiness. Fear and distrust keep us from living the life we were meant to live, and they are the greatest hurdles to seeing the truth about life—that it is good, abundant, supportive, and potentially joyous. *Trusting Life* is a deep exploration into the mystery of who we are, why we suffer, why we don't trust life, and how to become more trusting. It offers evidence that life is trustworthy and tools for overcoming the fear and beliefs that keep us from falling in love with life.

A Heroic Life: New Teachings from Jesus on the Human Journey. The hero's journey—this human life—is a search for the greatest treasure of all: the gifts of your true nature. These gifts are your birthright, but they have been hidden from you, kept from you by the dragon: the ego. *A Heroic Life* shows you how to overcome the ego's false beliefs and face the ego's fears. It provides you with both a perspective and a map to help you successfully and happily navigate life's challenges and live heroically. This book is another in a series of books dictated to Gina Lake by Jesus.

All Grace: New Teachings from Jesus on the Truth About Life. Grace is the mysterious and unseen movement of God upon creation, which is motivated by love and indistinct from love. *All Grace* was given to Gina Lake by Jesus and represents his wisdom and understanding of life. It is about the magnificent and incomprehensible force behind life, which created life, sustains it, and operates within it as you and me and all of creation. *All Grace* is full of profound and life-changing truth.

The Jesus Trilogy. In this trilogy by Jesus, are three jewels, each shining in its own way and illuminating the same truth: You are not only human but divine, and you are meant to flourish and love one another. In words that are for today, Jesus speaks intimately and directly to the reader of the secrets to peace, love, and happiness. He explains the deepest of all mysteries: who you are and how you can live as he taught long ago. The three books in *The Jesus Trilogy* were dictated to Gina Lake by Jesus and include *Choice and Will, Love and Surrender,* and *Beliefs, Emotions,* and *the Creation of Reality.*

For more info, please visit the "Books" page at
http://www.RadicalHappiness.com

Printed in Great Britain
by Amazon